Famous People

Queen Victoria

1819 – 1901

Sydney Wood

Sydney Wood has written numerous history
books for primary and secondary schools, as well
as books and articles for adults. He is a former
senior lecturer in history.

Picture credits
© Dorothy Burrows; Eye Ubiquitous/CORBIS: page 30 (top)
Getty Images/Hulton Archive: pages 8 (bottom), 18, 23, 30 (centre)
Liverpool Record Office, Liverpool Libraries: page 21
Mary Evans Picture Library: cover, page 27
McManus Galleries, Dundee City Council Leisure and Arts: pages 10, 11 (bottom)
© Michael Boys/CORBIS: page 30 (bottom left)
Tanworth Wells, *Victoria Regina* © Tate, London 2002: page 6
The Royal Collection © 2002, Her Majesty Queen Elizabeth II: pages 5, 8 (top), 13, 14, 24
V & A Picture Library: pages 11 (top), 30 (bottom right)

Published by 4Learning
124 Horseferry Road
London
SW1P 2TX
Tel: 08701 246 444
www.channel4.com/learning

© 2003 Channel Four Television Corporation

Author: Sydney Wood
Education Officer: Anne Fleck
Editor: Jackie Mace
Illustrator: Jacqueline Abrahams
Picture Researcher: Adelaide Kelly
Designer: Periscope Design Solutions
Printer: ESP Colour
Project Manager: Huw Jones
ISBN 186215983 1

Contents

The young princess

The Archbishop of Canterbury wanted to christen a baby girl. What was her name? He looked at her father and her father's older brother. 'Alexandrina' said the brother. 'Elizabeth' suggested the father. 'Certainly not,' said the brother, 'call her Alexandrina after Alexander, the ruler of Russia who is her godparent.' Seeing the baby's mother crying, he added, 'You may call her Victoria too, after her mother'. It was 24 June 1819. The baby grew up to become Queen Victoria.

Victoria's father, the Duke of Kent, was one of the King's younger sons. He died when she was only eight months old. Victoria did not have any brothers or sisters and lived with her mother, a German princess, in Kensington Palace. She did not go to school.

Some of the dolls that Victoria loved dressing

When Victoria was eight, tutors visited the palace to teach her history, geography, literature, religion and several foreign languages. A governess called Louise Lehzen looked after her. The governess was strict and when Victoria refused to do what she was told, she made her write down how naughty she had been in a 'behaviour book'.

As a child, Victoria enjoyed dancing, drawing and going to the theatre. Helped by her governess, she made clothes for some of her dolls (she had over 100). She liked to dress up her favourite pet spaniel called Dash, too.

Victoria's mother controlled her daughter's life very strictly. Victoria had to sleep in her mother's room even when, in 1837, she had her eighteenth birthday. However, 1837 was a special year in which the princess's life changed completely.

Victoria drew this portrait of herself in 1835.

Victoria's dog, Dash, wearing clothes the princess put on him

Becoming Queen

On the morning of 20 June 1837, Victoria was woken at 6 o'clock by her mother who said that the Archbishop of Canterbury and Lord Conyngham wished to see her. Later, Victoria wrote what happened in her diary. 'I went into my sitting room (only in my dressing gown) and alone. Lord Conyngham then acquainted [told] me that my poor uncle, the King, was no more and consequently that I am Queen.'

Now that she was 18 and Queen too, Victoria began to change her life. She moved out of her mother's bedroom and into her own private rooms. Very soon she moved to Buckingham Palace and put her mother in palace rooms far away from her own.

Victoria became Queen at a time when the royal family had been unpopular. However, she was only 18 and people were ready to wish her well.

Victoria being told she has just become Queen

She was crowned Queen in 1838. Half a million people turned out to see her travel to Westminster Abbey. The coronation service lasted for five hours and Victoria found that the royal crown she had to wear was very heavy. Afterwards, she changed out of her robes and bathed her dog, Dash, before having dinner. A splendid firework show ended the day.

Why Victoria became Queen

King George III died in 1820. He had several children including:

George
He became King George IV in 1820 but died ten years later. He did not have children to rule after him.

Frederick
He died in 1827 and did not have children who could succeed to the crown.

William
He became King William IV in 1830. He died in 1837 with no children to succeed him.

Edward
He was the Duke of Kent and died in 1820. His daughter, Victoria, became Queen in 1837.

What did the Queen do?

Lord Melbourne was Victoria's first Prime Minister.

Parliament agreed to pay the Queen a great deal of money every year. Over 400 people worked for the Queen and she had to pay them. They included the:

- ☞ **royal ratcatcher** – earned £80 a year.
- ☞ **fire and stovelighter** – earned £64 a year.
- ☞ **chimney sweep** – earned £111 a year.

Victoria worked hard. She met her government ministers and important foreign visitors, and read official papers. She was the head of the Church of England and helped to decide who should become bishops. Victoria had very strong views on what her government should do and made sure her ministers knew what she thought.

Victoria's Uncle Leopold, King of the Belgians, often wrote to her advising how she should behave. There were two ministers whom Victoria especially liked. When she first became Queen she trusted Lord Melbourne and cried when he had to hand over power to someone else. When she was older she enjoyed her meetings with Benjamin Disraeli. Both men listened to all the Queen said. They made her feel important and entertained her with stories.

Benjamin Disraeli was another of Victoria's Prime Ministers.

When Victoria became Queen, many people were not happy that Britain was ruled by a small number of rich people. They demanded change. By the time of Victoria's death, reforms meant that about two-thirds of adult men could vote in elections for parliament.

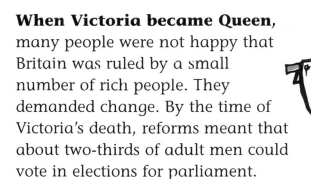

> *Women can't vote at all. We're paid half the wages men get and there are many jobs (like printing) that men keep to themselves.*

There were some changes in Victoria's time that improved women's lives. However, the Queen was not a strong supporter of allowing women to vote in elections for parliament.

Victoria's Britain

Life in Britain was changing when Victoria
became Queen. Britons led the world in inventing
machines that did work which had once been done by
hand. The machines were powered by steam engines
and placed in big buildings called factories. British
factories made things, like clothing, that were sent
all over the world.

Inside a Dundee mill

Other inventors developed railway lines. By 1847 these lines had spread all over the country. However, owners of stagecoach businesses were not pleased because people preferred to travel by rail as it was so much quicker. These changes meant that Britain became a richer and more powerful country.

In 1837, most British people lived in the countryside. By the time Queen Victoria died, around three-quarters of Britons lived in towns and cities. People moved to towns looking for work. Many of the houses they had to live in were very old or poorly built. For years, many people suffered from terrible illnesses that were caused by not having clean water to drink or proper lavatories. Many families just had one or two rooms to live in.

Rich children lived in big houses looked after by servants. They had lots of clothes and toys. But there were thousands of children who did not have enough clothes or enough to eat. Many children had to work because their parents needed the money that children earned. In Victoria's time, laws were passed to make children go to school, at least until they were twelve.

Children – from a poor home and from a wealthy home

'The Queen must marry'

Victoria's **Uncle Leopold** and Lord Melbourne told her she really should think about marrying. Britain needed the Queen to have a child to become the country's ruler when she died. But Victoria wasn't so sure.

" *But I'm used to having my own way, Lord Melbourne. So many of the princes are dull and plain. However, there is one man that I do really like.* "

There was one man that Victoria liked – Albert, the son of the duke of a little country (in what is now Germany) called Saxe-Coburg-Gotha. He was a little younger than Victoria. Albert was an intelligent and well-educated man who loved music. Victoria thought he was very handsome and very good at dancing.

Prince Albert

The Queen was so important that no one was allowed to ask her to marry them, so Victoria had to ask Albert. On 15 October 1839 she called Albert to her private room and he agreed to marry her. The Queen loved Albert very much and was glad to share her life with another young person. Marriage also meant she could tell her mother to leave the palace. Victoria and Albert married in February 1840 and had a three-day honeymoon at Windsor. Then Victoria said she had to return to work.

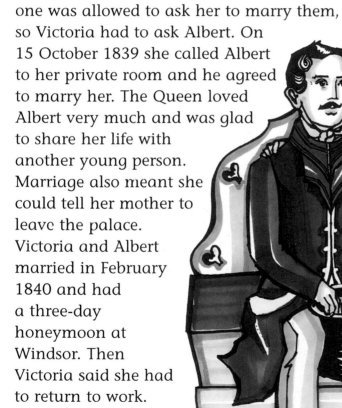

> *You know why I've asked you here. It will make me so happy if you will agree to what I want to happen.*

A happy marriage

Although she loved Albert, Victoria had a fierce temper if she did not get her own way. Albert stayed quiet when she shouted and screamed.

As the years passed, Victoria gave birth to nine children. This is one of many photographs that Victoria had taken. It shows the royal family. Starting from the left, the children's names were Alfred, Helena, Alice, Arthur, Beatrice (the baby), Victoria (the oldest), Louise, Leopold and Edward. Edward was the oldest boy, which meant he would be King when Victoria died.

Photography improved greatly during Victoria's reign. Cameras became much cheaper and easier to use. Victoria and Albert had their own camera and a special room at Windsor Castle where films could be turned into the final picture prints. Victoria used science in another way, too. She suffered a lot of pain when giving birth. When her eighth child was born she breathed in chloroform, poured on a handkerchief, to help ease the pain. It helped to make this treatment popular with other women, too.

This photograph was taken in 1857.

Victoria was a strict mother.
She did not spoil her children and
made sure they had simple meals.
Albert loved playing with the
royal children. He arranged for
tutors to come to teach them.
He was pleased to see how
clever Princess Victoria was.

Prince Edward, whom the
family called 'Bertie', a short
form of his first name 'Albert',
was a worry to his parents.
He would not listen to
his father or his tutor
and seemed just to
want to enjoy
himself. Albert sent
him to Oxford
University,
hoping that Bertie
would study harder
there.

*"Look here Bertie, you're at
Oxford to study. You really
must try harder."*

*"Life's for enjoying
yourself, Father.
Studying
bores me."*

CIGARS

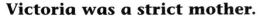

The Great Exhibition
of 1851 was Prince
Albert's idea. For the
Exhibition, Joseph Paxton
designed a huge glass
building called 'the Crystal
Palace'. Six million people
visited the Exhibition in
London. The railways made
it easy to get there. Objects
from forty different countries
were on display including
jewellery, leather goods,
textiles, china and
modern machinery.
The Queen visited
the Exhibition
many times.

Exhibition

Royal homes

Windsor Castle and Buckingham Palace were not proper family homes, so Victoria and Albert looked for somewhere they could really call their own. On the Isle of Wight they found a lovely area and bought some land. Albert planned their new home – Osborne House. In 1846 it was ready.

At Osborne House the princes learned to swim, sail, grow vegetables and make things from wood. The princesses played in a large wooden house that was built for them. They cleaned it, did the washing and learned to cook.

Victoria and Albert visited the Scottish Highlands and loved the area and the people. They bought land in Aberdeenshire and there, Albert helped a local architect to plan their home in Scotland – Balmoral Castle.

Osborne House

At Balmoral, the family went for walks and pony rides. Albert hunted deer and fished. Victoria painted and visited local people. Albert designed a new tartan. Victoria decorated Balmoral with tartan and the family wore kilts. The Queen did not seem to feel the cold and did not allow the rooms to be well heated. Visitors grumbled, but Disraeli managed to get a warm room by bringing a note from his doctor.

Albert wanted to improve ordinary homes too and made plans for better houses for workers. Two of his designs were built.

But some new buildings in Britain were far from comfortable. They were called workhouses and the people who lived in them hated them. Those too old or ill to work, and children whose parents had died, had to live in a workhouse if no one else would look after them.

~No Books.
~No Toys.
~No Card games.
~No Smoking.
~Husbands & Wives must be separate.

UNION

We've nowhere to live but in this cold, grim place.

19

Spare time

Victoria's children, like other rich children, had many toys. Clockwork toys became popular and children also played with model theatres and dolls' houses. Girls in rich families learned to paint, sing, play music and embroider – just like Victoria. They needed ways to fill their time because they were not expected to work when they grew up.

As Prince Edward grew up, he became very fond of going to horseraces and shooting at birds such as pheasants. His father, Prince Albert, loved stalking deer and sometimes shooting them. Many wealthy men went foxhunting, too. Victoria's sons did not go away to school, but many rich boys did. There they learned to play cricket and football.

Rich children played with model theatres.

20

The railways brought many changes to how people spent their free time. Rich people began to enjoy holidays in countries such as Switzerland. Many ordinary people used the railways too and went on day trips to places such as Blackpool. In Victoria's time, some workers began to have a whole week's holiday once a year.

Ordinary women had little spare time and were kept busy doing housework and other work to make some money. Football became more organised in Victoria's time, and men began going to watch it. Public houses were very popular with working men too, and many of them had singers to entertain customers. Men and women used to visit music halls to watch all sorts of different entertainers. By the end of Victoria's reign, some music halls had begun showing silent films, too.

This child earns a little money by entertaining men in public houses.

Fighting for the Queen

Victoria was proud of the British army and navy and sometimes wore military uniform to visit soldiers and sailors. The army fought a war against Russia in 1854–6 called the Crimean War. The Queen knitted socks and scarves for the soldiers. She would have liked to have gone to the war to help wounded soldiers, like Florence Nightingale did. She awarded a medal, called the Victoria Cross, to very brave soldiers who had fought in the Crimean War.

Soldiers called 'recruiting officers' travelled the country persuading young men to join the army. Soldiers were not well paid and their food was not very good. If they broke the army's rules they were punished very harshly. In 1870, many changes to the army began to improve it.

British soldiers and sailors had captured lands in many parts of the world. Victoria was very proud of this Empire, which included Canada, Australia, New Zealand and parts of Africa. She was especially interested in India. Disraeli persuaded Parliament to give the Queen the title of Empress of India. She had the huge Koh-i-noor diamond from India added to her crown.

The Queen with Disraeli, not long after she was made Empress of India

British soldiers had to fight in many parts of the world to increase and control the Empire. In 1857 they defeated Indian soldiers who did not want to be ruled by British people. In 1875, Britain gained control of the Suez Canal in Egypt, which was the quickest way to India. This led to soldiers fighting in Egypt to take control of the country.

Scottish Highland soldiers in Egypt in 1882

Alone

In 1861, **Prince Albert** became very ill with typhoid. On 14 December 1861, he died. The Queen was overcome with grief and for a time she would not see any of her ministers. She had Albert's room at Windsor Castle left as if he were still alive. For the rest of her life Victoria wrote all her letters on black-edged paper.

Many people at the time died from drinking water from wells and rivers that had sewage in them. In London, the River Thames smelled so much in 1858 that it was called 'the Great Stink'! The government began to organise improvements. By 1900 there were proper sewers in the towns and supplies of clean water, too.

For several years after Albert's death most people hardly ever saw the Queen. She withdrew from public life and spent her time at Osborne House or Balmoral, or abroad. People began to grumble that she was not doing her job.

The Queen and her daughter, Alice, by a statue of Prince Albert

At Balmoral, the Queen began to trust and rely on one of her staff on the estate – a man named John Brown, who had grown up on a farm in Scotland. Brown spoke to the Queen in a way her family and other servants did not like. If he did not like her clothes he would tell her. The Queen liked his honesty and became close to him. She brought him to Windsor and made him 'The Queen's Highland servant'. When he died in 1883 she was very sad.

Jubilee

Slowly Victoria recovered from her sadness. When Benjamin Disraeli was Prime Minister he did a great deal to persuade her to take part in public life again. Victoria preferred him to his great rival, William Gladstone. Gladstone wanted to give Ireland its own parliament. Victoria was against this and did her best to make life difficult for Gladstone.

The Queen in old age

Victoria was very fond of cakes and other sweet things and as the years went by, became quite fat. She ate quickly. Her guests found that when the Queen had finished eating, servants took away their plates too, even if they had not finished!

Her family increased until she had 38 grandchildren. She invited circuses to Windsor and Balmoral to entertain her family. She went out to the theatre and to Buffalo Bill's Wild West Show.

In 1887, the leaders of many countries in Europe came to London to celebrate Victoria's Golden Jubilee. Ten years later her Diamond Jubilee was held. This time the important people who came were from different parts of the huge British Empire which had been built up.

Queen Victoria died in 1901. She had ruled Britain for longer than any other king or queen and, during her reign, she had seen life change greatly. Her son, Edward, Prince of Wales, now became King. One of the first things he did was to clear out the rooms of Prince Albert and John Brown, which his mother had kept as if they were alive.

The Queen's Diamond Jubilee procession

A timeline of the Queen's life

Events in Victoria's life

1819	1830	1837	1840	1842	1851	1854

Victoria was born

King George IV died

Victoria became Queen

Victoria and Albert married

Victoria took her first railway trip

The Great Exhibition

Britain took control of Singapore

Manchester to Liverpool Railway officially opened

Samuel Morse showed how the electric telegraph worked

Penny post was set up

Grace Darling saved people in a shipwreck

Britain entered the Crimean War

Events in the world

Prince Albert died

Prince of Wales married

Victoria became Empress of India

John Brown died

Victoria's Golden Jubilee

Victoria's Diamond Jubilee

Victoria died

1861 **1863** **1876** **1883** **1887** **1897** **1901**

The first horse-drawn tram took to London

Football Association founded

Alexander Graham Bell invented the telephone

In Chicago, the first skyscraper was built

RAC founded

Royal Navy's first submarine launched

Remembering Victoria's time

There are many clues to Victoria's time all around us today.

A proper postal service began in Victoria's time.

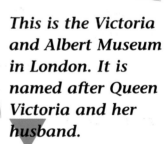

In towns and cities there are statues of Victorian people, including Queen Victoria.

This is the Victoria and Albert Museum in London. It is named after Queen Victoria and her husband.

Many buildings that we use today were built in Victorian times.

Glossary

Archbishop *(4)* A bishop of the highest rank.

Belgians *(8)* People who are born in Belgium.

chloroform *(14)* A chemical that helps to prevent pain.

clockwork *(20)* A machine with a spring that is wound up to drive a motor.

coronation *(7)* The ceremony of crowning a monarch.

elections *(9)* Voting for people to take up positions in parliament.

exhibition *(16)* A public display.

governess *(5)* A woman teacher employed by rich households to teach children.

honeymoon *(13)* A holiday taken by a newly married couple.

jubilee *(27)* A special anniversary that is celebrated.

kilt *(19)* A knee-length pleated skirt worn by Scottish men.

minister *(8)* The head of a government department.

palace *(4)* The home of a king or queen.

parliament *(8)* A group of elected people who represent a country.

Prime Minister *(8)* The head of parliament.

public house *(21)* A pub.

ruler *(12)* The head of a country.

spaniel *(5)* A breed of dog.

stagecoach *(11)* A horse-drawn vehicle formerly used to carry passengers.

tartan *(19)* A chequered pattern typical of Scotland.

typhoid *(24)* An illness caused by drinking dirty water.

workhouse *(19)* A place where very poor people lived.

Index

More books to read

Her Little Majesty: The Life of Queen Victoria by Carolly Erickson (Robson Books, 1999)

Queen Victoria by Juliet Gardiner (Collins and Brown, 1997)

Victorian Life by John Guy (Ticktock Media, 1997)

Victorian Scotland by Sydney Wood (Hodder & Stoughton, 1996)